THE
SAVORY PIE &
QUICHE
COOKBOOK

Disclaimer

Otherworld Publishing and its authors have used their best efforts in preparing these pages and their publications. Otherworld Publishing and its authors make no warranty of any kind, expressed or implied, with regard to the information supplied.

Limits of Liability

Otherworld Publishing and its authors shall not be liable in the event of incidental or consequential damages or injury in connection with, or arising out of, the providing of the information offered here.

Introduction

Savory pies and quiche are incredibly flavorful. They make a great dinner or lunch meal and are really easy to make!

Quiche are a naturally savory dish, created in an open pastry crust with moist custard, egg, cheese, meats, vegetables, or any combination thereof! It began as a French dish but has grown in popularity in many countries as an easy, delicious dish to be used for all occasions. Quiche are savory pies are pretty similar but savory pies are sometimes topped with crust and don't typically use custard in them.

In this cookbook you will find all kinds of delicious savory pies and quiches, all of which will tantalize your taste buds, wow your family and give you that quick, easy and delicious meal you've been looking for.

CONTENTS

QUICHE

ASPARAGUS QUICHE

This pretty dish is an excellent recipe for breakfast or brunch. Cook in advance and take to a party for an easy brunch addition!

Serves: 6 – 8

Ingredients:
½ lb. fresh asparagus, cut into ½" pieces
5 slices bacon, cooked and crumbled
1 – 8" pie crust, unbaked
1 egg white, beaten
2 eggs
¾ c. half and half
Nutmeg, salt and pepper to taste
1 c. shredded Swiss cheese

Method of Preparation:
1. Heat oven to 400 degrees
2. Place asparagus in steamer over 1" boiling water for about 5 minutes. Drain.
3. Brush pie shells with egg white and sprinkle bacon and asparagus into the shell.
4. In a bowl, beat the eggs, cream and seasonings. Sprinkle Swiss cheese over the bacon mixture, and then pour egg mixture on top.
5. Bake about 40 minutes in the oven.
6. Cook and serve!

Bacon Quiche Tarts

Who doesn't like bacon? These tarts can be made in advance, and can be reheated at any time in the oven. Just wrap in foil loosely and cook for 10 minutes at 350 degrees.

Serves: 8 - 10

Ingredients:
5 slices bacon, cooked and crumbled
1 – 8 oz. pckge cream cheese, softened
2 tbsp. milk
2 eggs
½ c. shredded swiss cheese
2 tbsp. chopped green onion
1 – 10 oz. can flake biscuit dough

Method of Preparation:
1. Preheat oven to 375 degrees. Grease 10 muffin cups
2. Mix cream cheese, milk and eggs in a bowl and beat until smooth. Stir in cheese and onions and set aside.
3. Separate the dough into 10 biscuits and press each into a muffin tin, covering the bottom and sides with a small rim. Sprinkle ½ the bacon evenly among the cups. Then add 2 tbsp. of the cream cheese mixture on top of the bacon.
4. Bake 20 to 25 minutes. When rims of tarts are golden brown, remove and sprinkle with remaining bacon.
5. Serve & enjoy!

BROCCOLI QUICHE

This quiche is not only delicious and easy, but looks beautiful on the table. It is light enough to be served at any meal but filling enough to leave you satisfied.

Serves: 6 – 8

Ingredients:
2 tbsp. butter
1 onion, chopped
1 tsp. garlic, minced
2 c. broccoli, chopped
1 – 9" pie crust
1 ½ c. mozzarella cheese, shredded
4 eggs, beaten
1 ½ c. milk
1 tsp. salt
½ tsp. pepper
1 tbsp. butter

Method of Preparation:
1. Preheat oven to 350 degrees
2. Melt butter in pan. Add garlic, onions and broccoli. Cook and stir until vegetables are tender. Place into crust and sprinkle cheese on top.
3. Mix eggs and milk, and add salt and pepper. Melt the butter and stir in. Pour over vegetables in pie crust.
4. Bake for 30 minutes.
5. Serve & enjoy!

CAPRESE QUICHE

This Quiche is Italian style and has amazing flavors of mozzarella, tomatoes and basil. Enjoy for breakfast or lunch for a sophisticated twist to the classic dish!

Serves: 6 – 8

Ingredients:
1 – 9" frozen pie crust
2 tbsp. olive oil
¼ c. diced onion
8 eggs
¼ tsp. lemon juice
10 leaves basil, chopped
Salt & Pepper to taste
2 tomatoes, diced
1 -12 oz. package fresh mozzarella

Method of Preparation:
1. Preheat oven to 350
2. Heat oil in a pan over medium heat. Cook onion until softened.
3. Reduce heat to low and cook and stir for about 15 minutes more, until onion is softened and dark brown.
4. Spread cheese and tomatoes on the bottom of the pie crust. Mix eggs, lemon juice, basil, salt & pepper and onions in a bowl. Pour into the pie crust.
5. Bake for 30 – 40 minutes, until eggs are set.
6. Serve & Enjoy!

CARROT CASHEW QUICHE

This recipe is very unique and combines delectable flavors that will impress any crowd. Serve it hot or cold, and add a crisp salad for a light meal sure to please.

Serves: 6 – 8

Ingredients:
½ c. butter
1 c. sliced carrots
1 c. cashews
½ c. honey
3 eggs
1 ½ c. heavy cream
½ tsp. nutmeg
½ tsp. salt
¾ c. shredded cheddar cheese
1 – 9" pie crust

Method of Preparation:
1. Preheat oven to 350 degrees
2. Melt butter in a pan and stir in carrots and cashews. Cook until carrots are tender and cashews turning brown. Mix in honey.
3. Beat the eggs, heavy cream, nutmeg and salt in a bowl.
4. Spread the cheese in the bottom of the pie crust. Place carrot mixture on top of cheese and add egg mixture.
5. Bake 40 minutes.
6. Serve & enjoy!

CHEDDAR QUICHE

This quiche is easy and delicious. With simple ingredients, a small kick of flavor, and a shorter baking time, it is a great one to use as a quick family dinner that the kids will love.

Serves: 6 – 8

Ingredients:
1 – 9" frozen pie crust, unbaked
3 slices bacon, chopped
1 onion, chopped
2 c. shredded cheddar cheese
4 eggs
1 tsp. salt
¼ tsp. hot pepper sauce
1 – 12 oz. can evaporated milk, heated through

Method of Preparation:
1. Heat oven to 400 degrees.
2. Place bacon and onion in a skillet over medium heat and cook until bacon is browned. Drain and crumble the bacon into the pie shell. Add onions and cheddar cheese.
3. In a bowl, beat eggs with the salt and hot sauce and slowly stir in evaporated milk. Pour into the pie pan.
4. Bake 5 minutes, and then reduce heat to 350 degrees and bake for 25 minutes. The quiche will set more as it cools.
5. Enjoy!

CORN TORTILLA QUICHE

This quiche has a crispy tortilla crust that gives it a feel of a taco with the taste of a quiche. Delicious for any meal of the day, it is easy and fun to make!

Serves: 6 – 8

Ingredients:
¾ lb. bulk pork sausage
5 – 6" corn tortillas
1 c. shredded Monterey Jack cheese
1 c. shredded Cheddar cheese
¼ c. chopped green chiles
6 eggs, lightly beaten
½ c. heavy whipping cream
½ c. ricotta cheese
½ tsp. chili powder
¼ c. fresh cilantro, chopped

Method of Preparation:
1. Preheat oven to 350 degrees and lightly grease 9" pie dish
2. Cook sausage in skillet over high heat until crumbly and brown. Drain grease.
3. Place 4 tortillas in pie plate, overlap them ½ inch past the edge of the pan. Place final tortilla in center of pan. Place sausage, cheese, and green chilies over the tortillas.
4. Whisk eggs, cream, ricotta cheese and chili powder together and pour over the sausage mixture.
5. Bake about 45 minutes until center is set.
6. Sprinkle with cilantro and enjoy!

CRAB QUICHE

This Crab Quiche can be delicious for brunch or even a tasteful dinner! Real or imitation crab meat can be used and the hot sauce can be adjusted to your tastes!

Serves: 6 – 8

Ingredients:
1 – 9" frozen pie crust
4 eggs
1 c. heavy cream
½ tsp salt
½ tsp pepper
Hot Sauce – optional amount
1 c. shredded Monterey Jack cheese
¼ c. shredded parmesan cheese
1 – 8 oz. package of crab meat
1 green onion, diced

Method of Preparation:
1. Preheat oven to 350
2. Bake the pie crust for 10 minutes & remove
3. In a bowl, whisk the eggs, cream, salt and pepper and hot sauce.
4. Stir in cheese, onion and crab.
5. Pour into the pie shell and bake for 30 minutes in oven.
6. Turn off the oven, but leave the door closed and quiche in place for an additional 20 minutes. This makes for a creamier texture!
7. Serve & Enjoy

CRUSTLESS QUICHE

This healthier version of a quiche allows the delicious flavors without the added calories and carbs of a crust. Adjust ingredients to your taste and enjoy!

Serves: 6 - 8

Ingredients:
1 ½ tsp. olive oil
5 green onions, diced
2 tsp garlic, minced
1 – 6 oz bag baby spinach
1 ½ tsp. olive oil
8 mushrooms, sliced
4 eggs
8 oz. feta cheese, crumbled
1 lb. spicy cheese, shredded

Method of Preparation:
1. Preheat oven to 325 degrees.
2. Heat 1 ½ tsp oil in an oven safe pan. Cook green onions and garlic in oil for 1 minute. Stir in spinach, cover and cook about 5 minutes. Transfer to a large bowl
3. Heat 1 ½ tsp. oil in the same pan and cook mushrooms until lightly browned. Remove from heat.
4. Remove excess moisture from spinach by squeezing, and then stir into mushrooms. Whisk eggs in a bowl until mixed and add to spinach mixture. Stir in feta and spicy cheese.
5. Transfer mixture back into pan. Bake in the oven for about 45 minutes.
6. Cut and enjoy!

HAM & WILD RICE QUICHE

This recipe makes a change up from normal quiche with lots of veggies and wild rice. It's unique flavor makes it a great meal at any time.

Serves: 6 - 8

Ingredients:
1 c. cooked wild rice
1 – 9" unbaked pie crust
1 c. cubed ham, cooked
1/3 c. red bell pepper, chopped
¼ c. green onion tops, sliced
1 – 4 oz. can mushrooms, sliced
3 eggs, beaten
1 c. sour cream
1 tbsp. dijon mustard
½ tsp. salt
1/8 tsp. pepper
2 c. Swiss cheese, shredded

Method of Preparation:
1. Preheat oven to 425 degrees. Bake pie crust 10 minutes and then reduce heat to 400.
2. Mix the rice, ham, peppers, onions and mushrooms in a bowl. Separately, mix eggs, sour cream, mustard and seasonings.
3. Place 1 c. swiss cheese in pie crust. Spread the rice, ham and veggie mix over the top and cover with the egg mixture. Top with remaining cheese.
4. Bake 30 minutes and remove. Let stand 10 minutes.
5. Serve & Enjoy!

HAMBURGER QUICHE

Adding hamburger to Quiche turns this normal brunch food into a hearty dinner. Filling and delicious, it will please all those at your dinner table!

Serves: 6 – 8

Ingredients:
1 – 16 oz. pckge frozen hash browns, thawed
½ lb. ground beef
1 onion, chipped
1 c. milk
2 eggs, lightly beaten
1 tbsp. cornstarch
½ lb. sharp cheddar, grated
¼ tsp. liquid smoke
1 – 3 oz. jar bacon bits
2 tsp. Worcestershire sauce
¼ lb. cheddar cheese, grated

Method of Preparation:
1. Preheat oven to 350 degrees and lightly grease 9" pie dish
2. Press hash browns into pie dish tightly and bake for 25 minutes in oven.
3. Put ground beef and onion in a large pan. Cook until beef evenly browns. Drain and allow to cool.
4. In a bowl, whisk together milk, eggs and cornstarch. Stir in the ½ lb. shredded cheese and ground beef. Stir in bacon bits, liquid smoke, and Worcestershire sauce.
5. Pour over hash browns
6. Bake for 20 minutes in oven, remove and sprinkle remaining cheese. Put back oven for 15 minutes. Let stand 20 minutes before serving.
7. Eat and enjoy!

MEXI-QUICHE

Refried beans and a chorizo layer give this quiche a Mexican food twist that is delicious and unexpected. You can heat the beans slightly beforehand to make spreading easy.

Serves: 6 – 8

Ingredients:
1 – 9" pie crust
10 oz. chorizo sausage
6 eggs
¼ c. milk
1 – 10 oz. can tomatoes diced with green chili peppers
2 c. Mexican shredded cheese, divided
1 – 15 oz. can refried beans

Method of Preparation:
1. Preheat oven to 400.
2. Heat a pan over medium heat. Cook chorizo until brown and crumbly. Drain grease.
3. Beat eggs and milk in a bowl. Stir in tomato mixture and half the cheese.
4. Spread the beans across the bottom of the pie crust.
5. Spread chorizo on top of the refried beans and then pour egg mixture on top. Spread remaining cheese on top of the mixture.
6. Bake about 45 minutes, until toothpick inserted into middle comes out clean.
7. Let stand for 15 minutes before serving.
8. Enjoy!

MINI-QUICHE

Mini-Quiche recipes provide an easy and fun way to serve a delicious meal to a group of people. Take these to any party for an instant hit. You can garnish with olives!

Serves: 6 – 8

Ingredients:
12 slices bread
1 onion, chopped
½ c. Swiss cheese, shredded
1 c. milk
4 eggs
1 tsp. dry mustard
¼ tsp. black pepper

Method of Preparation:
1. Preheat oven to 375 degrees. Grease 12 muffin tins
2. Cut bread into circles Place on bottoms of muffin tins. Sprinkle the onion and cheese evenly among the muffin tins.
3. Mix milk, eggs, mustard and pepper in a bowl until combined. Divide evenly amount muffin tins.
4. Bake for 20 minutes.
5. Serve and enjoy!

MOREL QUICHE

Morel mushrooms give this quiche a unique flavor. With heavy whipping cream, it is a fluffy and delicious meal at any time!

Serves: 6 – 8

Ingredients:
1 – 9" pie crust
1 tbsp. butter
1 onion, chopped
½ c. cooked ham, chopped
1 c. morel mushrooms
4 eggs
1 c. heavy whipping cream
1 tbsp. flour
½ c. Monterey jack cheese, shredded

Method of Preparation:
1. Preheat oven to 350
2. Heat butter in a pan until melted. Mix in onion and ham until onion is tender, about 5 minutes. Stir in mushrooms and cook, stirring frequently, for 2 minutes.
3. Bake pie crust in oven for approx. 10 minutes, until slightly browned.
4. Whisk eggs with cream and flour until mixed. Stir in cheese.
5. Spread ham and mushroom combination into pie crust and pour egg mixture on top.
6. Bake for 45 minutes until the filling is set!

ONION QUICHE

This Quiche provides a tasty but versatile flavor. It can be used as a base for other quiches, a side dish for just about any meal, or a great meal on its own.

Serves: 6 – 8

Ingredients:
1 – 9" frozen pie crust
1 tbsp. butter
1 onion, diced
3 eggs
1/3 c. heavy cream
1/3 c. shredded swiss cheese

Method of Preparation:
1. Preheat oven to 375
2. Melt butter in a saucepan. Add onions and cook until soft, about 5 minutes
3. In a bowl, mix the eggs and cream. Stir in the cheese.
4. Spread the onions on the bottom of the pie crust, and pour the egg mixture over the onions.
5. Bake for 30 minutes.
6. Serve & Enjoy!

QUICHE SEVILLE

This quiche is easy and sophisticated. With bacon and sour cream mixed in, it produces a flavor that everyone will be sure to love.

Serves: 6 – 8

Ingredients:
1 – 9" pie crust, thawed
1 c. sour cream
10 slices bacon, crumbed
1 c. shredded Monterey Jack cheese
2 ¾ oz french fried dried onions
6 eggs, lightly beaten
½ tsp. Worcestershire sauce

Method of Preparation:
1. Preheat oven to 375 degrees
2. Bake pie shell for 10 minutes, then remove and reduce oven to 350 degrees.
3. In a bowl, combine sour cream, bacon, cheese, French-fried onions, Worcestershire sauce, and eggs together. Once mixed well, pour into the cooled pie shell.
4. Bake for 35 to 45 minutes until center is set.
5. Serve & Enjoy!

RICE CRUST FOR QUICHE

If you are looking for a healthier and unique crust to substitute in any quiche recipe, use this delicious rice crust as your base!

Serves: 1- 9" pie crust

Ingredients:
1 c. water
1 c. instant rice
1 tbsp. butter
Cooking spray

Method of Preparation:
1. Boil water in a small saucepan. Add rice, cover and remove from heat. Allow to stand until water is absorbed, about 5 minutes. Stir in butter.
2. Grease a 9" pie pan. Spoon the rice into the pan. Press the rice firmly against the pan with the back of your spoon to create a crust.
3. Fill with quiche recipe of your choice and bake as directed!

SALMON QUICHE

For those who don't love turkey or ham, this salmon dish can easily be a delicious substitute. You can make 2 and freeze one for later! Serve with fresh veggies like asparagus for an amazing dinner.

Serves: 6 – 8

Ingredients:
1 – 9" pie crust, thawed
1 – 8 oz. package cheddar cheese block. Cubed.
¼ onion, chopped
4 eggs
1 – 12 fluid oz. can evaporated milk
Salt & Pepper to taste
¼ tsp. garlic powder
¼ tsp. dried parsley
¼ tsp. dried sage
1 – 14.75 oz can salmon, drained, remove bones
½ c. shredded cheddar cheese, divided

Method of Preparation:
1. Preheat oven to 375 degrees
2. Place cubed cheddar cheese, onion, eggs and milk into blender. Add seasonings and blend until smooth and mixed.
3. Spread salmon into pie crust. Sprinkle ¼ c. shredded cheddar cheese over the salmon, and pour the egg mixture in. Top with remaining cheese.
4. Bake for 30 minutes, or until set
5. Serve & Enjoy!

᛫ SHRIMP QUICHE

This can be made on its own or as an accompaniment to the prior Salmon Quiche for a seafood quiche buffet! It can be served cold or hot.

Serves: 6 – 8

Ingredients:
1 – 9" pie crust, baked
4 oz. small cooked shrimp (peeled & deveined)
2/3 c. Gruyere Cheese
2 eggs, lightly beaten
1 c. sour cream
1 tbsp. green onion, chopped
Salt & Pepper

Method of Preparation:
1. Preheat oven to 350 degrees
2. Spread shrimp across pie crust and sprinkle with cheese
3. Stir the sour cream, onion and salt and pepper into the eggs and pour over the cheese/shrimp
4. Bake for 30 minutes
5. Serve and enjoy!

Spinach Artichoke Quiche

The artichoke in this recipe adds a delicious, almost tart flavor to the recipe. The full tomato slices create a beautiful dish that will look good on any table.

Serves: 6 - 8

Ingredients:
1 – 9" unbaked pie shell
4 eggs
5 slices bacon, cooked & crumbled
½ c. mozzarella cheese, shredded
2 tbsp. milk
2 tbsp. flour
2 tsp. garlic, minced
1 tsp. parsley
½ tsp. thyme
1 c. spinach, divided
½ c. artichoke hearts, chopped
2 plum tomatoes, sliced

Method of Preparation:
1. Preheat oven to 350 degrees.
2. Mix eggs, bacon, mozzarella, milk, flour, and spices together.
3. Place ½ of spinach on bottom of pie crust. Sprinkle the artichoke hearts over the spinach. Pour eggs on top. Place remaining spinach over eggs, and top with tomato slices.
4. Bake about 45 minutes until center is set.
5. Enjoy!

SPINACH QUICHE

This is one of the most traditional forms of quiche and is always a crowd-pleaser. It is a forgiving recipe that can be customized to your tastes and desires!

Serves: 6 – 8

Ingredients:
½ c. butter
3 tsp. garlic, minced
1 onion, chopped
1 – 10 oz. package frozen spinach, chopped, thawed and drained
1 – 4.5 oz. can mushrooms
1 – 6 oz. pckge herb feta, crumbled
1 – 8 oz. pckge shredded cheddar cheese
Salt & pepper to taste
1 – 9" pie crust, unbaked
4 eggs, beaten
1 c. milk

Method of Preparation:
1. Heat oven to 375 degrees.
2. Melt butter in a pan over medium heat. Sauté garlic and onion until brown, about 8 minutes.
3. Stir in the spinach, mushrooms, feta and ½ c. cheddar cheese. Season with salt and pepper.
4. Pour into pie crust.
5. In a medium bowl, beat eggs and milk together lightly. Season with more salt & pepper, and pour over vegetable mixture in pie crust.
6. Base in oven for 15 minutes. Sprinkle with the remaining cheese and bake an additional 40 minutes.
7. Serve and enjoy!

TOMATO, KALE & LEEK QUICHE

For the health lover, this crustless quiche is filled with vitamins from veggies. Make it at night and reheat for an easy, healthy breakfast.

Serves: 6 - 8

Ingredients:
1 c. kale, chopped & steamed
1 leek, sliced (green & white parts only)
4 oz. cherry tomatoes, halved
4 eggs
1 c. milk
4 oz. Italian Cheese mix, shredded
1 sprig rosemary, chopped
¼ tsp. salt
1 tbsp. parmesan cheese, shredded

Method of Preparation:
1. Preheat oven to 375 degrees. Grease an 8" pie crust
2. Place cooked kale in pie crust. Add sliced leek and the tomatoes.
3. In a bowl, mix eggs with milk and Italian cheese. Then stir in rosemary and salt.
4. Pour eggs over veggies in pie dish. Stir until the two mixtures are combined.
5. Bake about 30 minutes. Remove and top with parmesan cheese. Continue to bake for 20 more minutes.
6. Serve and Enjoy!

ULTIMATE QUICHE

This quiche is very creamy and filling. It can be frozen for later after baking, and any combination of meats that you can think of can be used or substituted.

Serves: 6 – 8

Ingredients:
1 – 9" frozen pie crust, unbaked
1 ½ tsp. green bell pepper, chopped
½ onion, diced
¼ c. mushrooms, chopped
3 eggs
1 c. heavy cream
¼ lb. shredded Monterey Jack cheese
¼ lb. shredded Swiss cheese
6 oz. cooked ham, chopped
¼ tsp. vinegar
¼ tsp. tarragon
Pinch of garlic powder
Pinch of ground nutmeg
Salt & Pepper to taste

Method of Preparation:
1. Heat oven to 350 degrees and cook pie crust for 10 minutes
2. In a pan, sauté green pepper, onions and mushroom until translucent
3. In a large bowl, mix eggs and cream. Add in cheeses, ham and sautéed vegetables. Stir in the vinegar and season with herbs. Pour into pie crust
4. Bake for 55 to 60 minutes
5. Serve and enjoy!

VEGETABLE QUICHE

This Quiche is made for vegetarians. It provides a great light breakfast or lunch and can be served hot or cold!

Serves: 6 – 8

Ingredients:

1 tsp. salt	1 tsp. garlic, minced
½ c. zucchini, chopped	¼ tsp. curry powder
1 – 9" pie crust, unbaked	Salt & Pepper to taste
2 tbsp. butter	¼ tsp. ground cinnamon
1 ½ c. onion, chopped	5 eggs
1 green bell pepper, chopped	¼ c. milk
1 c. tomatoes, chopped	¼ c. parmesan cheese, shredded
½ c. mushrooms, sliced	¼ c. cheddar cheese, shredded

Method of Preparation:

1. Sprinkle tsp. of salt over zucchini and let sit to drain for 10 minutes.
2. Preheat oven to 350.
3. Bake pie shell for 10 minutes
4. Melt butter in pan over medium heat. Cook onion, green peppers, tomatoes, mushrooms zucchini and minced garlic until tender. Stir in curry powder, salt & pepper, cinnamon and transfer into the pie crust.
5. Beat the eggs in a bowl with milk and all cheese. Pour over the vegetables.
6. Bake for 40 – 45 minutes. Let stand for 5 minutes before serving.
7. Enjoy!

WEEK NIGHT QUICHE

This quiche is easy and fast. It uses crescent rolls as the crust for a light, flaky crust! Because it is not a traditional pie shell, cooking time is greatly reduced.

Serves: 6 – 8

Ingredients:
1 – 8 oz. pckge crescent roll dough
2 slices ham
½ c. roasted red peppers, chopped
1 – 10 oz. pckge frozen spinach, chopped and thawed
½ c. shredded cheddar cheese
6 eggs
3 tbsp. milk
Salt & Pepper to taste
1 splash hot sauce

Method of Preparation:
1. Heat oven to 350 degrees
2. Unroll the crescent dough into one piece. Line an 8x8 baking dish (it will extend over slightly). Prick the dough throughout with a fork.
3. Bake crust in oven about 10 minutes until golden
4. Layer the ham, peppers, spinach and cheese over the crust. Beat eggs, milk, salt & pepper and hot sauce in a bowl and pour into the pan.
5. Bake for 15 minutes. Turn oven to broil and cook for a few minutes more until top is slightly browned.
6. Cool and enjoy!

SAVORY PIES

ARTICHOKE PIE

You can use this recipe for a main dish or an appetizer. It is always enjoyed and is very easy to make at any time!

Serves: 6 - 8

Ingredients:
1 tbsp. olive oil
1 tsp. garlic, minced
2 – 6 oz. cans artichoke hearts
½ c. Italian bread crumbs
½ c. parmesan cheese, divided
1 9" pie crust
3 eggs, beaten
1 – 8 oz. pckge mozzarella cheese, grated

Method of Preparation:
1. Preheat oven to 350 degrees
2. Heat oil in a skillet and saute garlic until it starts to brown. Add artichoke hearts and cook 10 minutes. Add the bread crumbs and ½ the parmesan cheese. When heated all through and mixed, place half of the mixture into the crust.
3. Pour the eggs of the artichoke mixture and the rest of the parmesan cheese. Add the rest of the artichoke mixture and top with mozzarella.
4. Bake for 45 minutes!

BACON PIE

A bacon pie can be eaten at breakfast, lunch or dinner for a savory and tasty meal.

Serves: 6 - 8

Ingredients:
12 slices bacon
1 c. swiss cheese, grated
1/3 c. onion, chopped
2 c. milk
4 eggs
1 c. baking mix
1/8 tsp. black pepper

Method of Preparation:
1. Heat oven to 400 degrees. Grease a 9" pie plate
2. Cook bacon until brown, drain & dry and crumble.
3. Spread bacon, cheese and onion into the dish.
4. Mix the milk, eggs and baking mix with pepper in a small bowl. Pour over the bacon mixture.
5. Bake 40 minutes.
6. Serve and enjoy!

BBQ PIE

With baked beans and ground beef all under a crust, this dish is a perfect summer recipe to share with the whole family!

Serves: 6 - 8

Ingredients:
1 ½ lbs. ground beef
¼ c. onion, chopped
¼ tsp. pepper
2 – 15 oz. cans baked beans with pork
1 tsp. Worcestershire sauce
1 c. bbq sauce
1 c. biscuit baking mix
½ c. milk
1 egg
¼ c. cheddar cheese, shredded
1 tbsp. bbq sauce

Method of Preparation:
1. Preheat oven to 350 degrees
2. Brown ground beef in a skillet with onion and pepper. Drain grease.
3. Stir in baked beans, Worcestershire sauce and 1 c. bbq sauce. Place in a large casserole dish. Separately, mix the baking mix, milk and egg. Pour over the beef mixture.
4. Bake for 45 minutes. Spread a small amount of bbq sauce over the top and sprinkle with cheddar cheese while hot.
5. Enjoy!

BEAN PIE

This makes 2 pies that can be used at any time as a main dish or as a perfect party pie to be shared by a large group.

Serves: 6 - 8

Ingredients:
1 tbsp. vegetable oil
1 onion, chopped
1 green bell pepper, chopped
1 – 15 oz. can black beans, drained
1/3 c. salsa
¼ c. red bell pepper, chopped
¾ tsp. chili powder
¼ tsp cayenne pepper
2 – 9" pie shells
1 ½ c. cheddar cheese, grated

Method of Preparation:
1. Preheat oven to 325 degrees
2. Heat oil in a pan. Add onions and peppers and cook until tender. Stir in the beans, salsa, and seasonings and simmer for 15 minutes.
3. Spoon half into each pie crust and cover with cheese.
4. Bake for 1 hour!

BEEF & BISCUIT PIE

With biscuits, ground beef, and onion this dish is the definition of savory. Substitute cheese flavorings to mix up the flavor.

Serves: 6 - 8

Ingredients:

1 ¼ lb. ground beef

½ c. onion, chopped

¼ c. green chile peppers, chopped

1 – 8 oz. can tomato sauce

2 tsp. chili powder

½ tsp. garlic salt

1 – 10 oz. can buttermilk biscuit dough

½ c. sour cream

1 ½ c. Monterey Jack cheese, shredded & divided

1 egg beaten

Method of Preparation:

1. Preheat to 375 degrees
2. Brown ground beef, onion and green chili peppers in a pan. Add in the tomato sauce, chili powder and garlic. Mix and bring to simmer.
3. Pull the biscuits apart into 10 biscuits, and then pull each biscuit in half. Place 10 halves on the bottom of a pie dish to form the bottom crust.
4. Ad ½ c. cheese, sour cream and egg to meat mixture and then pour over crust. Add the last biscuit halves to the top in a layer. Sprinkle remaining cheese on top.
5. Bake for 30 minutes.
6. Enjoy!

CAULIFLOWER CHEESE PIE

This recipe makes cauliflower extremely flavorful and delicious! With a potato crust it is a filling and healthy meal.

Serves: 6 - 8

Ingredients:

2 c. shredded potatoes
¼ c. onion, chopped
1 egg, beaten
1 tsp. salt
1 tbsp. flour
1 ½ tbsp. olive oil
1 tbsp. vegetable oil
1 onion, chopped

2 tsp garlic, minced
½ tsp. basil
½ tsp. thyme
1 head cauliflower, chopped
1 ½ c. cheddar cheese, grated
2 eggs, beaten
¼ c. milk
¼ tsp. paprika

Method of Preparation:
1. Preheat oven to 400 degrees and grease a 9" pie plate
2. In a bowl, combine potatoes, onion, egg, salt and flour. Transfer into pie pan and press firmly. Bake for 30 minutes. Brush with oil and bake an additional 10 minutes. Remove and reduce oven heat to 375 degrees.
3. In a pan, heat oil and sauté onion, garlic basil and thyme with paprika until softened. Add cauliflower and cook for 15 minutes.
4. Spread ½ of the cheese onto the crust, then spread the vegetables on top. Add remaining cheese on top. Mix the milk and eggs and then pour over the top of the mixture.
5. Bake for 35 to 40 minutes and enjoy!

CHICKEN POT PIE

This pie made from scratch will impress any company! It is hearty, savory and filling and a perfect meal for a winter or fall evening.

Serves: 6 - 8

Ingredients:

1 lb. skinless/boneless chicken breast, cubed
1 c. carrots, sliced
1 c. frozen green peas
½ c. celery, chopped
1/3 c. butter
1/3 c. onion, diced

1/3 c. flour
½ tsp. salt
¼ tsp. pepper
¼ tsp. celery seed
1 ¾ c. chicken broth
2/3 c. milk
2 -9" pie crusts

Method of Preparation:

1. Preheat oven to 425 degrees
2. Place chicken, carrots, peas and celery into a large saucepan. Cover with water and boil for 15 minutes. Drain and set mixture aside
3. In the same pan, cook butter and onions until soft. Stir in the flour, salt/pepper and celery seed. Slowly mix in the chicken broth and milk. Simmer until thick. Remove from heat.
4. Place the chicken mixture in one pie crust. Pour the broth mixture on top. Cover with the second pie crust. Seal edges and make small slits in the top to vent.
5. Bake for 35 minutes. Cook for 10 minutes.
6. Serve & Enjoy!

CHILES RELLENOS PIE

You will find this warm and comforting in the winter but light enough for a summer dinner! Delicious Mexican flavor will make this a dinner favorite.

Serves: 6 - 8

Ingredients:
6 poblano chile peppers
2 c. Monterey jack cheese, grated
2 c. cheddar cheese, grated
1 ½ c. cooked chicken, diced
4 tbsp. flour
1 c. evaporated milk
1 c. sour cream
3 eggs
2 c. salsa

Method of Preparation:
1. Preheat oven on boiler setting. Roast the poblano chiles on a cookie sheet until the skin is charred on all sides. Cool and peel off skin. Remove the stem and seeds. Turn oven temperature to 350 degrees.
2. Line an 11" baking dish with the peppers. Add cheeses evenly over the peppers. Spread the cooked chicken on top. Mix the flour with a small amount of the evaporated milk until a paste forms, then whisk in the remaining milk and sour cream. Beat in eggs. Pour over the chicken.
3. Bake for 40 minutes and spread salsa on the top. Bake an additional 15 minutes.
4. Enjoy!

EASY POT PIE

This may be the easiest version of pot pie available. Throw this together anytime you need a warm dinner in a flash.

Serves: 6 - 8

Ingredients:
3 tbsp. butter, melted
1 -1 6 oz. package frozen veggie mix
1 – 5 oz. can chicken chunks (drained)
2 – 10.75 oz. cans cream of chicken soup
½ c. milk
1 – 10 oz. can refrigerated layer biscuits

Method of Preparation:
1. Preheat to 425 degrees. Butter a pie dish with melted butter, reserving 1 tbsp.
2. Cook vegetables and chicken in a pan over medium heat until tender. Add soup and milk. Mix until well combined and smooth. Bring to a boil.
3. Take off stove and spread into the pie pan. Place the biscuits in small layers on top of mixture. Drizzle the remaining butter on top.
4. Bake for 15 minutes.
5. Enjoy!

ENGLISH COTTAGE PIE

This is a traditional mince pie from England. It has mashed potatoes added s a crust to make it a filling pie. Serve with peas for a traditional meal.

Serves: 6 - 8

Ingredients:
1 lb. ground beef
1 onion, chopped
3 carrots, chopped
2 tbsp. flour
½ tsp. ground cinnamon
1 tbsp. Italian Seasoning
2 tbsp. parsley, chopped
1 ½ c. beef broth
1 tbsp. tomato paste
4 potatoes, peeled and cubed
¼ c. butter, softened
1 c. milk
¼ c. cheddar cheese, shredded

Method of Preparation:
1. Preheat to 400 degrees
2. Cook ground beef with onion and carrot until browned. Add flour, cinnamon, Italian seasoning and parsley.
3. In a bowl, mix beef broth and tomato paste. Add to beef. Simmer for 15 minutes. Spoon into 9 inch pie plate
4. Boil potatoes until tender. Drain.
5. Mash with butter and milk and whip until fluffy in consistency. Spread over the beef.
6. Sprinkle with cheese and bake for 25 minutes.
7. Enjoy!

FISHERMAN PIE

For a seafood savory pie, use this recipe for a delectable treat. It makes your house smell amazing and gives the fish an amazing flavor with a garlic/lemon sauce.

Serves: 6 - 8

Ingredients:
Crust:
3 potatoes, cubed & peeled
3 tbsp. butter
1 tsp. nutmeg
1 tsp. cayenne pepper
½ c. milk
Spinach:
2 tsp. olive oil
12 oz baby spinach
Sauce:
3 tbsp. butter
3 tbsp. flour
2 tsp. garlic, minced
2 c. cold milk
2 tsp. lemon zest
Remaining:
1 tbsp. butter
1 tsp. cayenne pepper
2 lbs. boneless cod fillets
½ lemon, juiced
1 tbsp. chives, chopped

Method of Preparation:

1. Boil potatoes in water until tender. Drain, and mash with butter. Add nutmeg and cayenne pepper. Mix in ½ c. milk into the potato mixture.
2. Cook spinach and olive oil in a pan over high heat about 2 minutes, until spinach is wilted. Place in a bowl with a paper towel to drain excess moisture.
3. Heat 3 tbsp. butter and flour in pan. Mix quickly into paste and stir constantly until it is slightly browned .Add garlic and stir quickly for about 10 minutes.
4. Whisk in 1 c. milk into the flour mixture. Once thickened, add remaining 1 c. milk and lemon zest. Bring to simmer, stirring constantly and then turn heat very low and let sit.
5. Heat oven to 375 degrees. Grease a casserole dish with 1 tbsp. butter.
6. Season the pan with salt, pepper and cayenne. Place cod fillets in a single layer and season with more salt, pepper & cayenne. Spread spinach over the top and drizzle with lemon. Add white sauce on top.
7. Spread the mashed potato mixture evenly on the top.
8. Bake until bubbling, about 40 minutes.
9. Broil for 2 minutes until top is slightly crusty.
10. Garnish with chives and enjoy!

French Canadian Tourtiere

This is a traditional meat pie that is usually served on Christmas Eve!

Serves: 6 - 8

Ingredients:
1 lb ground pork
½ lb ground beef
1 onion, chopped
1 tsp. garlic, minced
½ c. water
1 ½ tsp salt
½ tsp thyme
¼ tsp. sage
¼ tsp. pepper
1/8 tsps ground cloves
1 – 9" pie crust

Method of Preparation:
1. Preheat oven to 325 degrees
2. Combine pork, beef, onion, garlic water and seasonings in a pan. Cook until boiling, stirring occasionally. Simmer for 5 minutes more and then allow to cool.
3. Place the meat mixture into the pie shell. Cover with 2nd crust and seal. Slit on top to vent the steam.
4. Cook for 35 minutes.
5. Serve and enjoy!

FRENCH LEEK PIE

This is an old French recipe used during the holiday season. It is great with a salad any time of year! It can be prepared early and eaten cold any time.

Serves: 6 - 8

Ingredients:
1 – 9" pie shell, thawed
2 tsp. butter
3 leeks, chopped
Salt & pepper to taste
1 c. light cream
1 ¼ c. gruyere cheese, shredded

Method of Preparation:
1. Preheat oven to 375 degrees
2. Melt butter in a pan, and stir in leeks. Cook for about 10 minutes until tender. Add salt and pepper. Stir in cream and the cheese and cook until it is warm all the way through. Pour into the pie shell.
3. Bake for 30 minutes.
4. Enjoy!

IRISH STOUT PIE

For your guests to feel full and satisfied, there is no better meal than this Irish classic. With steak, bacon and beer, it is a medley of delicious flavors.

Serves: 6 - 8

Ingredients:

2 – 9" pie crusts
2 lbs round steak, cubed
1 tbsp. flour
3 oz. lard
8 slices bacon, cooked and crumbled

5 onions, diced
1 c. mushrooms, sliced
1 – 12 oz bottle Irish stout beer
1 tbsp. chopped parsley
1 tsp. brown sugar

Method of Preparation:
1. Preheat to 325 degrees
2. Place lard in pan and heat to melted.
3. While melting, roll steak cubes into flour and add to melted lard. Cook until browned, about 10 minutes.
4. Move steak to a casserole dish.
5. Cook onions and mushrooms in the same pan until tender. Add to steak mixture.
6. Stir in beer, parsley and brown sugar, and cover the dish with aluminum foil.
7. Bake about 2 ½ hours until steak is tender.
8. Remove from oven and increase temperature to 400 degrees.
9. Bake bottom pie crust about 10 minutes.
10. Remove, and add steak mixture to pie crust. Add second pie crust to top and seal edges.
11. Bake about 10 to 15 minutes until golden brown.
12. Enjoy!

MEATLOAF PIE

Meatloaf is a traditional and favorite family dish. Use this pie recipe to combine the meatloaf and mashed potatoes for one simple dish!

Serves: 6 - 8

Ingredients:
1 – 9" pie crust
1 lb. ground beef
1 onion, chopped
1 egg
1 tbsp. ketchup
1 tbsp. Worcestershire sauce
1 – 8.75 oz. can kernel corn
2 c. mashed potatoes
½ c. cheddar cheese, grated

Method of Preparation:
1. Preheat to 350 degrees
2. Brown ground beef with onion in a pan. Drain grease
3. Mix the beef mixture, egg, ketchup and Worcestershire in a bowl.
4. Place the corn in the bottom of the pie shell, add beef mixture and spoon mashed potatoes on top. Layer cheese on top.
5. Bake 30 minutes.
6. Enjoy!

MEDITERRANEAN PUFF PASTRY CHICKEN

Chicken with flavors of garlic, sun-dried tomatoes and cheese all in a flaky puff pastry is a delicious and elegant meal!

Serves: 4

Ingredients:
3 tbsp. garlic, minced
1 egg yolk
2 c. spinach, chopped
2 boneless, skinless chicken breast halves
2 tbsp. basil pesto
1/3 c. sun-dried tomatoes, chopped
¼ c. feta cheese, crumbled
1 puff pastry sheet, thawed and cut in half

Method of Preparation:
1. In a bowl, mix garlic and egg yolk. Spread over the chicken breasts on both sides. Refrigerate for 4 hours or overnight to marinate flavorings.
2. Preheat oven to 375 degrees and grease a cooking sheet.
3. Put one half of the puff pastry sheet on a floured board. Add ½ c. spinach in the center of the sheet. Place one chicken breast on top of spinach. Add 1 tbsp. pesto on top, then add sun-dried tomatoes and ½ the feta cheese and finally top with ½ c. more spinach. Fold the pastry sheet up and around the mixture, sealing tightly. Place seam side down on cooking sheet. Repeat with second chicken breast.
4. Bake 50 minutes
5. Enjoy!

MEXICAN SHEPHERDS PIE

This is a south of the border version of the popular American Pot Pie. Add a salad for a delicious and easy meal!

Serves: 6 - 8

Ingredients:
1 ½ lb ground beef
1 onion chopped
1 tsp garlic powder
1 – 14.5 oz. can diced tomatoes
1 package taco seasoning mix
¾ c. hot water
1 – 11 oz. can whole kernel corn
1 – 8.5 oz. package corn muffin mix
1 c. cheddar cheese shredded
1 – 2.25 oz. can black olives

Method of Preparation:
1. Preheat to 400 degrees and grease a 9x13 baking dish
2. Cook beef and onion in a pan until beef is brown. Drain the grease.
3. Mix in garlic and tomatoes and cook for 5 additional minutes. Mix in taco seasoning and water, and allow to simmer for 5 minutes. Add to baking dish and top with corn.
4. Prepare corn muffin mix as directed and spread evenly over the mixture in the baking dish.
5. Bake 20 minutes.
6. Garnish with olives and cheese and enjoy!

MUSHROOM PIE

This pie is surprisingly creamy and rich. The dill adds a surprising flavor and the bacon and cream make it feel comforting and aromatic!

Serves: 6 - 8

Ingredients:
1 tbsp. olive oil
1 – 10 oz. pckge mushrooms sliced
1 onion, diced
4 slices bacon, chopped
¾ c. heavy cream
1 c. swiss cheese, grated
1 tsp. fresh dill, chopped
1 – 17.25 oz. pckge puff pastry (thawed)
1 egg, beaten lightly

Method of Preparation:
1. Preheat to 350 degrees
2. Heat oil in pan and cook mushrooms, onion and bacon until tender. Reduce the heat and add cream and dill. Cook for 10 minutes more. Remove from heat and mix in the cheese.
3. Lay one sheet of puff pastry on a baking sheet (well oiled) and pour mushroom mix on top. Cover with the second sheet and seal the edges together. Poke a few holes in the top with a fork.
4. Brush the beaten egg over the top.
5. Bake 40 minutes until brown.
6. Cool and cut into squares. Enjoy!

QUICK CHEESEBURGER PIE

For a traditional and well-liked meal, cheeseburgers are a perfect go to, and this recipe lets you cook all in one pie instead of individual patties.

Serves: 6 - 8

Ingredients:
1 – 9" pie shell, thawed
1 lb. ground beef
1 onion chopped
1 tsp garlic, minced
½ tsp salt
¼ c. flour
1/3 c. dill pickle juice
1/3 c. cold milk
½ c. chopped dill pickles
2 c. swiss cheese, shredded

Method of Preparation:
1. Heat oven to 425 degrees
2. Brown ground beef with onion and garlic. Drain grease.
3. Add salt and ¼ c. flour to beef mixture. Mix in pickle juice, milk, pickles and 1 c. cheese. Transfer into pie shell.
4. Bake for 15 minutes, then sprinkle with remaining cheese and bake 5 minutes.
5. Enjoy!

SHEPHERD'S PIE

This pie is layered with beef, carrots and potatoes and makes a delicious and hearty meal. Eat for dinner or serve earlier in the day for lunch for a filling meal!

Serves: 6 - 8

Ingredients:

4 potatoes, peeled and cubed
1 tbsp. butter
1 tbsp. onion, chopped
¼ c. cheddar cheese, shredded
5 carrots, sliced
1 tbsp. vegetable oil.

1 onion, chopped
1 lb. ground beef
2 tbsp. flour
1 tbsp. ketchup
¾ c. beef broth
¼ c. cheddar cheese, shredded

Method of Preparation:

1. Boil a pan of water and add potatoes. Cook until tender, about 15 minutes. Drain and mash
2. Mix in butter, 1 tbsp. onion and ¼ c. cheese. Set aside.
3. Boil a second pan of water and add carrots. Cook about 15 minutes, until softened. Drain and mash. Set aside.
4. Preheat oven to 375 degrees.
5. Cook onion in small amount of oil until tender and clear. Add ground beef and cook until browned. Drain fat, and then stir in flour and cook 1 minute. Add ketchup and beef broth. Heat to a boil, then reduce to low and simmer for 5 minutes.
6. Spread the beef mixture on the bottom of a casserole dish. Spread the mashed carrots on top. Next, tope with mashed potatoes and sprinkle remaining cheese on top.
7. Cook for 20 minutes until just golden brown.
8. Serve & Enjoy!

STEAK PIE

This hearty meal is a traditional Scottish dish. Made to keep you full and happy, it is warm and delicious!

Serves: 6 - 8

Ingredients:
1 tbsp. vegetable oil
1 lb. beef stew meat
1 onion, chopped
½ c. beef stock
1 c. water
1 tsp. Worcestershire sauce
1 sheet frozen puff pastry, thawed

Method of Preparation:
1. Preheat oven to 400 degrees
2. Heat oil in a pan and cook meat until browned on the outside. Add in onion and cook until softened. Mix in the beef stock and water, and add Worcestershire and seasonings. Simmer for 20 to 30 minutes.
3. Put the beef mixture into a casserole dish. Top with the puff pastry sheet. Press the edges onto the dish to form a seal.
4. Bake for 20 minutes.
5. Enjoy!

TACO PIE

Taco pie is a quick, fun meal that cab be served as a family dinner or set out at a party for everyone to take a bit of. It is flavorful and easy!

Serves: 6 - 8

Ingredients:
1 – 8 oz. package crescent roll dough
1 lb. ground beef
1 package taco seasoning mix
1 – 16 oz. sour cream
8 oz. mexican style cheese, shredded
1 – 14 oz. bag tortilla chips, crushed

Method of Preparation:
1. Preheat to 350 degrees
2. Lay crescent rolls out in a square cake pan and bake for the amount of time directed on crescent roll packaging
3. Brown ground beef in a pan over medium heat. Add taco seasoning and mix. Place meat mixture on top of cooked crescent rolls. Add sour cream and cheese in layers, and top with crushed chips.
4. Bake for 10 minutes
5. Serve & enjoy!

TOMATO PIE

This will make you feel like you're eating a BLT sandwich but even better! Use whatever cheese is your favorite.

Serves: 6 - 8

Ingredients:
1 – 9" pie crust
5 tomatoes, peeled & sliced
½ c. basil, chopped
3 green onions, sliced
½ lb bacon, cooked and chopped
½ tsp. garlic
1 tsp. oregano
2 c. cheddar cheese (or other favorite), shredded
¼ c. mayonnaise

Method of Preparation:
1. Preheat to 375 degrees
2. In layers, alternating, place tomatoes, basil, green onions, bacon, garlic, and oregano in pie shell. Mix cheese with mayo in a bowl and spread into pie shell. Cover with aluminum foil.
3. Bake for 30 minutes. Remove foil and bake an additional 30 minutes.
4. Enjoy hot or cold!

TURKEY POT PIE

This recipe gives a great way to use leftover turkey after Thanksgiving. You can even freeze the baked pie to use later!

Serves: 6 - 8

Ingredients:

2 – 9" pie crusts
4 tbsp. butter, divided
1 onion, chopped
2 celery stalks, diced
2 carrots, sliced
3 tbsp. parsley
1 tsp. oregano

2 cubes chicken bouillon
2 c. water
3 potatoes, peeled & cubed
1 ½ c. turkey, cubed and cooked
3 tbsp. flour
½ c. milk

Method of Preparation:
1. Preheat to 425 degrees
2. Melt 2 tbsp. butter in a pan and cook celery, onion and carrots until tender. Add in the parsley and oregano.
3. Stir in bouillon and water. Bring to a boil and add potatoes. Cook for about 15 minutes, until just tender.
4. Melt remaining butter in a pan. Mix in turkey and flour. Add milk and cook until heated through. Add the turkey mix to the vegetable mixture and cook about 5 minutes. Pour into the bottom pie shell. Roll the top shell onto the top, seal edges and add a few cuts on top for steam.
5. Bake for 15 minutes. Reduce oven to 350 degrees and continue to bake for 20 minutes.
6. Enjoy!

VEGETABLE POT PIE

This pie is incredibly easy to prepare. The kids will love the familiar flavors of cream soup and you will love all the vegetables!

Serves: 6 - 8

Ingredients:
1 – 10.75 oz. can condensed cream of potato soup
1 – 15 oz can mixed vegetables
½ c. milk
½ tsp. thyme
½ tsp. pepper
2 – 9" pie crusts, thawed
1 egg, beaten

Method of Preparation:
1. Preheat to 375 degrees
2. Mix potato soup, vegetables, milk, and seasonings in a bowl.
3. Add to bottom pie crust. Cover with second crust and seal edges. Vent the top and brush with the beaten egg
4. Bake for 40 minutes
5. Serve & Enjoy!

Made in the USA
Las Vegas, NV
04 November 2022

58769985R00037